Raccoons

Written by
Jill Atkins

This little critter is a raccoon.

You might spot raccoons in forests and near rivers.

This is all good habitat for them.

A raccoon has thick silver fur and black rings on its long tail.

Can you see the black patterns?
Do you think it looks like a robber?

A raccoon is bigger than a cat.

This raccoon is grabbing the cat food from the dish.

This raccoon **is** a robber!

A raccoon has ten fingers, just like us.

Its fingers help it to grip a tree trunk. Then it can clamber up the tree.

It likes to sit high up in the tree.

Its fingers help it to get food as well.

It can pick up nuts and crack them with its teeth.

Raccoons can swim well.

They like to be near rivers and ponds.

Then they can grab the fish that flicker and flash along.

Raccoons like rain, but they do not like thunder or lightning.

So they need to shelter from a storm. They might shelter in a drain.

What do you think a raccoon might have in its lunchbox?

It might have fish, frogs, insects, eggs, snails, nuts …

... and little things like rabbits, squirrels and rats.

If raccoons are starving, they might look for food in rubbish bins.

But they must not crunch on plastic or crisp bags. That is so bad for them!